Nita Mehta's

VEGETARIAN

Microwave

COOKBOOK

COOKING, BAKING AND GRILLING IN THE MICROWAVE

Nita Mehta's

VEGETARIAN

Microwave

COOKBOOK

COOKING, BAKING AND GRILLING IN THE MICROWAVE

100% TRIED & TESTED RECIPES

Nita Mehta

**B.Sc. (Home Science), M.Sc. (Food and Nutrition)
Gold Medalist**

Tanya Mehta

SNAB
Publishers Pvt Ltd

Nita Mehta's
VEGETARIAN
Microwave
COOKBOOK

Reprint 2008

ISBN 81-7869-069-1

Food Styling & Photography: **SNAB**

Layout and laser typesetting:

National Information
Technology Academy
3A/3, Asaf Ali Road
New Delhi-110002
☎ 23252948

Picture on cover:	**Anjeeri Gobhi** **Rice-Vegetable Ring**
Picture on page 1:	**Paneer Tikka**
Picture on page 2-3:	**Ghiya-Channe ki Dal** **Paneer Makhani**
Picture on page 4:	**Vegetable au Gratin**
Picture on page 94:	**Soya Kebabs**
Picture on back cover:	**Chocolate Walnut Cake**

Published by:

SNAB
Publishers Pvt Ltd
3A/3 Asaf Ali Road
New Delhi-110002

Editorial and Marketing office:
E-159, Greater Kailash-II, N.Delhi-48
Tel: 91-11-23250091, 23252948, Fax: 29225218
Tel: 91-11-29214011, 29218727, 29218574
E-Mail: nitamehta@email.com, nita@nitamehta.com
Website: http://www.nitamehta.com
Website: http://www.snabindia.com

Printed at:

BRIJBASI ART PRESS LTD.

Distributed by:

THE VARIETY BOOK DEPOT
A.V.G. Bhavan, M 3 Con Circus
New Delhi - 110 001
Tel: 23417175, 23412567; Fax: 23415335

Price: Rs. 195/-

Introduction

The microwave helps today's women facing time constraints, to prepare a variety of favourite delicacies in a faster and a simpler manner. It leaves her with more time to spend with the family. Microwave makes the cooking simpler as the food does not stick or burn and hence it does not need constant stirring. The food is cooked and served in the same dish, so there is less washing up to do. This efficient equipment not only reheats food but also boils, bakes, thaws and skewers, making cooking interesting and enjoyable. Microwave with its multiple advantages not only makes cooking much more fun, but also helps retain the food's nutritive value.

Cooking with microwave energy, is different from the conventional cooking. Microwaves are a form of high frequency electromagnetic waves which penetrate the food and execute the molecules inside, to vibrate at high speed. This causes friction and heat is produced thereby cooking the food very fast. The vitamins, the natural aroma and juices are retained, which invariably tends to get lost in conventional cooking. As the food is cooked in its own juices, very little oil or fat is used in cooking.

The recipes have been adapted to suit the Indian palate. This book covers a range of vegetarian recipes, starting from starters to soups to main course Indian, Continental, Chinese and Thai dishes. A few desserts, some which turn out even better in a microwave than the conventional cooking, like our favourite "Gajar ka Halwah" have been made very simple to cook in a microwave. Look forward to these wonderful recipes and share it with those you love and care about!

Nita Mehta's

CONTENTS

SNACKS & STARTERS   16

SOUPS   29

INDIAN CURRIES

INDIAN DRY AND MASALA   50

RICE   67

CHINESE AND THAI   71

CONTINENTAL AND BAKED DISHES   80

DESSERTS AND CAKES   88

Basics of Microwave Cooking

Timing: Set the timings carefully, foods can become hard and leathery, if overcooked. It is always better to undercook than to overcook in a microwave. The larger the volume of food there is, the more timing is needed to cook it. 4 potatoes cook in 6 minutes, whereas 8 potatoes cook in about 9 minutes. Therefore, if the quantity in a recipe is

changed, an adjustment in timing is necessary. When doubling a recipe, increase the cooking time 50% approximately and when cutting a recipe in half, reduce time by about 40%.

Standing time: Food continues to cook for sometime, even after it is removed from the microwave. For example, the cake cooked in a microwave looks very moist and undone when removed from the oven after microwaving it for the specified time, but after it is left aside for 8-10 minutes, it turns perfect.

Covering: Covers are used to trap steam, prevent dehydration, speed cooking time, and help food retain its natural moisture. When covering with paper napkins, a good microwave cooking practice, be sure to use a double width that will enable you to tuck the paper under the bottom of the cooking dish. Otherwise, it will tend to rise off the dish due to the air movement. A handy idea to keep in mind; a heatproof china plate is a good substitute for a lid. For shorter cooking time (within 6 minutes) cling films can also be used.

Stirring: If necessary, stir from the outside to the center because the outside area heats faster than the center when microwaves are in use. Stirring blends the flavours and promotes even heating. Stir only as directed in the recipes, constant stirring is never required, frequent stirring is rare.

Arrangement: The microwaves always penetrate the outer portion of food first, so food should be arranged with the thicker areas near the edge of the dish and the thinner portions near the center. Chicken/Mutton should be so placed that the meaty part is towards the outside. Food such as tomatoes, potatoes and corn should be arranged in a circle, rather than in rows.

Microwave Tips

- Never over-cook food as it becomes tough and leathery. Give the dish a little standing time before you test it, to avoid over cooking.

- Never pile food on top of each other. It cooks better, evenly and quickly when spaced apart.

- Food cooks better in a round container than in a square one. In square or rectangular bowls, the food gets overcooked at the corners.

- Do not add salt at the time of starting the cooking as it leads to increase in the cooking time.

- Do not add more water than required, however a little water must be added to prevent dehydration of the vegetables. When the vegetables get dehydrated, there is a loss of natural juices as well. But addition of extra water increases the cooking time.

- Do not deep fry in a microwave (the temperature of oil cannot be controlled).

- Do not cook eggs in their shells (pressure will cause them to explode).

- Do not cook and reheat puddings having alcohol (they can easily catch fire).

- Do not use containers with restricted openings, such as bottles.

- Use deep dishes to prepare gravies, filling the dish only ¾ to avoid spillage.

- Do not use aluminium foil for covering dishes in the microwave mode. Do not reheat foods (sweets like *ladoos, burfi* etc.) with silver sheet, as it leads to sparking.

- When using the convec mode put the dish on the wire rack to get even baking.

- Always preheat the oven when you want to use the convec mode. Grilling does not need preheating.

- When making *tikkas* or other tandoori delicacies cover the plate beneath the rack with aluminium foil to collect the drippings.

Interesting Uses of a Microwave

- Making ghee. Keep 1½ - 2 cups malai (milk topping) in a big glass bowl and microwave on high for 15-20 minutes to get desi ghee without burning your kadhai (wok). Stir once or twice inbetween.

- Blanching almonds to remove skin. Put almonds in a small bowl of water and microwave for 3 minutes or till water just starts to boil. After the water cools, the almonds can be peeled very easily.

- Freshening stale chips, biscuits or cornflakes. Place the chips or biscuits in a napkin, uncovered, for about 1 minute per bowl or until they feel warm. Wait for a few minutes to allow cooling and serve.

- Boiling (actually microwaving) potatoes. Wash potatoes and put them in a polythene bag. Microwave high for 5 minutes for 4 medium potatoes.

- Making khatti mithi chutney. Mix 1 tbsp amchur, 3 tbsp sugar, some water along with spices in a glass bowl. Microwave, stirring in between.

- Warming baby's milk bottle. Do check the temperature of the milk on your inner wrist. The bottle will not become hot, while the milk will.

- Softening too-hard ice cream, cream, cheese and butter.
- Making dry bread crumbs from fresh bread. Crumble the slice of bread and microwave the bits of slices for 2-3 minutes. Mix once and microwave further for another minute or two. Give some standing time to the moist bread to dry out and then grind in a mixer to get crumbs.
- Drying herbs. Fresh parsley, dill (soye), mint (poodina), coriander (dhaniyan), fenugreek greens (methi) — all greens can be dried in a microwave, preserving the green colour. Give them some standing time to turn dry. Use them in raitas and curries.
- Melting chocolate, butter, jam, honey, etc. Dissolving gelatine.
- Sterilizing jars for storing home made jams and pickles.
- Freshening stale bread by placing 2 slices between the folds of a paper and microwaving for 20 seconds. It turns absolutely soft and the stale bread becomes perfect for sandwiches.
- To roast 1 tbsp of cashews spread on a microproof plate and microwave for 1 minute to get golden roasted cashews.
- To roast papad place 2 papads on a paper napkin and microwave for 1½ minutes. Turn side once inbetween.
- To blanch 4 tomatoes, put a cross at the stem end of each tomato. Place tomatoes on a microproof plate and microwave for 2 minutes. Peel after they cold down.
- To cook corn, wash a corn on the cob and place in a plastic bag microwaver for 2-3 minutes to get soft corn.
- To boil ½ kg arbi wash and put in a plastic bag. Microwave for 11 minutes, turning once inbetween.

Utensils used in the Microwave Oven

MODE	CAN USE	DO NOT USE
Microwave Round or oval dishes are better for this mode as the corners of the square dish absorb more microwave energy or rays and hence food at the corners tends to get over cooked.	China Pottery (earthenware) Heatproof glass dishes like pyrex, borosil etc. Paper and cloth napkins as covers Plastic or cling wrap can be used as cover for short durations. Wooden skewers and toothpicks Plastic or polyethylene cooking bags.	China or any other utensil with gold or silver lining. Very delicate glass dishes Metal cake tins or any other metal Aluminium foil as covers Metal skewers
Convection In this mode there are no microwave rays or microwave energy. The oven becomes a conventional oven when put on this mode so all utensils which go in the regular oven work well in the microwave oven when set on the convection mode.	Metal cake tins or any other metal utensil Heat proof glass dishes like pyrex of borosil Metal skewers Aluminium foil as covers	Delicate glass dishes which are not heatproof Wooden skewers Paper and cloth napkins or plastic wraps
Grill In this mode there are no microwaves so all heatproof utensils work well.	All as given for convec mode	All as given for convec mode
Combination (Micro+Oven) (Micro+Grill) Utensils must be microproof as well as heatproof for both the combination modes	Heat proof glass dishes like pyrex or borosil Use a glass microproof and heatproof glass plate as cover	Metal tins China Utensils Wooden and metal skewers Aluminium foil, paper or cloth napkins or plastic wrap.
Combination (Grill+Oven) Utensils must be heatproof	All as given for convec mode	All as given for convec mode

Snacks & Starters

Bean Squares

A quick Mexican starter - crackers topped with cheesy beans and roasted peanuts.

Serves 4

8 cream cracker biscuits
½ cup grated cheese
½ cup boiled rajmah (red kidney beans)
2 tbsp tomato sauce
½ tsp salt, ¼ tsp red chilli powder
2 green chillies - deseeded, finely chopped
½ tsp oregano, ½ tsp salt
a few roasted peanuts

SOUR CREAM
2 tbsp fresh cream - chilled
½ cup thick dahi (yogurt) - hang for 15 minutes in a muslin cloth & squeeze lightly
½ tsp lemon juice, ¼ tsp salt, or to taste
¼ tsp pepper, preferably white pepper

1. For the sour cream, beat curd till smooth. Gently mix lemon juice, cream, salt and pepper. Keep sour cream in the refrigerator till serving time.
2. Mix cheese, boiled rajmah, tomato sauce, salt, red chilli powder and chopped green chillles. Keep topping aside till serving time.
3. To serve, spread 1 tbsp full of the bean topping on each biscuit in a heap, leaving the edges clean.
4. Place a paper napkin on the glass plate in the microwave.
5. Keep all the cream cracker biscuits together on it and microwave at 60% power for 3 minutes.
6. Serve each biscuit with a blob of sour cream and then top with a peanut.

17

Italian Mushroom Caps

Mushroom stuffed with a filling flavoured with Italian dressing.

Serves 4

**200 gm mushroom
1 tbsp olive oil
½ onion - finely chopped
1 bread slice - remove sides and churn in a mixer to get fresh crumbs
1 tbsp chopped coriander
1 tbsp grated pizza cheese
salt and pepper to taste**

**WHISK TOGETHER
2 tbsp olive oil, 1 tbsp vinegar
½ tsp garlic paste, ¼ tsp salt, ¼ tsp pepper**

1. Wash mushroom and hollow out the mushroom by removing the stem. Scoop out a little more with a melon scooper. Pat dry on a kitchen towel.
2. Whisk olive oil, vinegar, garlic, salt and pepper. Rub this flavoured oil on the inside and outside of each mushroom.
3. Chop the mushroom stems finely and mix in the left over flavoured olive oil mix.
4. Microwave 1 tbsp olive oil, chopped stems and onion for 2 minutes.
5. Add bread and coriander. Mix well. Add salt, pepper to taste.
6. Fill each mushroom with this filling, forming a little heap.
7. Pierce a wooden toothpick from the side of each mushroom. Keep aside till serving time.
8. To serve microwave stuffed mushrooms for 4 minutes.
9. Sprinkle mozzarella cheese and again microwave for 30 seconds or till cheese melts slightly.

Pav Bhaji

Mixed vegetables flavoured with a fragrant spice blend. Enjoy it as a snack or for dinner.

Serves 4

3 onions - chopped finely
3 potatoes
2 carrots - peeled and chopped
½ cup peas
1½ cups chopped cauliflower
1 cup chopped cabbage
3 tbsp oil
3 tbsp butter
2 tsp ginger-garlic paste
2½ tbsp pav bhaji masala
¼ tsp haldi (turmeric powder)
1½ tsp salt
3 tomatoes - chopped
1 tbsp chopped coriander

1. Wash potatoes. Put in a plastic bag and microwave for 5 minutes. Peel and mash coarsely.
2. In a deep microproof bowl, put carrots, peas, cauliflower and cabbage. Add ½ cup water. Mix and microwave for 8 minutes. Let it cool. Blend roughly in a mixer for 1-2 seconds. Do not make it into a paste.
3. In a microproof dish add 3 tbsp oil, onions, ginger-garlic paste, 2 tbsp pav bhaji masala and haldi. Mix well. Microwave for 6 minutes.
4. Add tomatoes and the roughly mashed vegetables. Mix well. Add 2 tbsp butter, 1½ tsp salt. Cover and microwave for 10 minutes. Stir once in between.
5. Add 1 cup water. Mix and microwave for 5 minutes.
6. Add 1 tsp pav bhaji masala, 2 tbsp chopped coriander and 1 tbsp butter. Mix and serve.

Sesame Gold Coins

Sesame seeds and vegetables on golden brown bread, dotted with some tomato ketchup.

Picture on facing page   *Servings 12*

6 bread slices
butter enough to spread
2 potatoes
1 small onion - chopped finely
1 carrot - chopped finely (diced)
1 capsicum - chopped finely (diced)
½ tsp soya sauce, 1 tsp vinegar
½ tsp pepper, ¼ tsp chilli powder
salt to taste
sesame seeds (til) - to sprinkle
chilli garlic tomato sauce to dot

1. Wash potatoes. Put in a plastic bag and microwave for 4 minutes. Peel and mash coarsely.
2. In a dish microwave onion and oil for 3 minutes. Add carrot and capsicum. Microwave for 2 minutes.
3. Add potatoes, soya sauce, vinegar, salt, pepper and chilli powder. Microwave for 2 minutes.
4. With a cutter or a sharp lid, cut out small rounds (about 1½" diameter) of the bread. Butter both sides of each piece lightly.
5. Spread some potato mixture in a slight heap on the round piece of bread, leaving the edges clean. Press. Sprinkle sesame seeds. Press.
6. Set your microwave oven at 180°C using the oven (convection) mode and press start to preheat oven.
7. Place gold coins on grill rack.
8. Re-set the preheated oven at 180°C for 12 minutes. Cook till bread turns golden on the edges and turns crisp from the under side. Serve, dotted with chilli-garlic sauce.

Sweet Corn Soup: Recipe on page 30, Sesame Gold Coins ➢

Instant Khaman Dhokla

This light Gujarati snack is quick to make in a microwave.

Serves 6   *Picture on opposite page*

1½ cups besan (gram flour)
1 cup water, 1 tbsp oil
½ tsp haldi (turmeric)
1 tsp green chilli paste, 1 tsp ginger paste
1 tsp salt, 1 tsp sugar
¼ tsp soda-bi-carb (mitha soda)
1½ tsp eno fruit salt, 2 tsp lemon juice

TEMPERING
2 tbsp oil, 1 tsp rai (mustard seeds)
2-3 green chillies - slit into long pieces
¼ cup white vinegar
¾ cup water, 1 tbsp sugar

1. Grease a 7" diameter round, flat dish with oil. Keep aside.
2. Sift besan through sieve to make it light and free of any lumps.
3. Mix besan, water, oil, turmeric powder, salt, sugar, chilli paste, ginger paste and water to a smooth batter.
4. Add eno fruit salt and soda-bi-carb to the batter and pour lemon juice over it. Beat well for a few seconds.
5. Immediately pour this mixture in the greased dish. Microwave uncovered for 6 minutes. Remove from oven and keep aside.
6. To temper, microwave oil, green chillies, rai, water, sugar and vinegar for 4½ minutes. Pour over the dhokla and wait for ½ hour to absorb it and to turn soft.
7. Cool and cut into 1½" pieces.
8. Sprinkle chopped coriander. Serve.

Chutney Submarine

Mango chutney spread on a loaf of bread and topped with some salad and paneer roundels.

Serves 4-5

1 long French bread - cut lengthwise
2 tbsp butter - softened
2 tbsp sweet mango chutney
1 cucumber - cut into round slices without peeling
2 firm tomatoes - cut into round slices
a few poodina (mint) leaves to garnish
400 gm paneer, 2 tbsp oil
¼ tsp haldi, ½ tsp chilli powder
½ tsp salt, 1 tsp chaat masala powder

1. Cut paneer into ¼" thick slices and then into round pieces with a biscuit cutter or bottle cover or into squares.
2. Sprinkle paneer on both sides with some chilli powder, salt, haldi, chaat masala and oil. Grill for 10 minutes.
3. Spread butter on the cut surface of both the pieces of french bread, as well as a little on the sides.
4. Set your microwave oven at 180°C using the oven (convection) mode and press start to preheat oven.
5. Place bread on grill rack in the hot oven. Re-set the preheated oven at 180°C for 12 minutes. Cook till bread turns crisp.
6. Apply 2 tbsp mango chutney on the buttered side.
7. Sprinkle some chaat masala on the cucumber and tomato pieces.
8. Place a piece of paneer, then cucumber, then tomato and keep repeating all three in the same sequence so as to cover the loaf. Place them slightly overlapping. Insert fresh mint leaves in between the vegetables, so that they show. Serve at room temperature.

Soya Kebabs

Serves 4   *Picture on page 94*

1 cup soya granules (nutri nugget granules)
100 gm paneer - grated (1cup)
2 bread slices - torn in small pieces and churned in a mixer to get fresh crumbs
1 tsp garam masala, 1 tsp salt
½ tsp red chilli powder
1½ tbsp tomato ketchup
2 tbsp chopped green coriander - finely chopped
1 green chilli - chopped finely

1. Soak granules in 1 cup water for 15 minutes.
2. Strain, squeeze out the water well from the soya granules.
3. Add paneer, fresh bread crumbs, garam masala, salt, red chilli powder, tomato ketchup, chopped green coriander or mint and green chilli to the soya granules. Mix very well.
4. Make balls of the mixture. Flatten each ball to get a kebab, with oiled hands.
5. Place on the grill of the oven. Spoon 1 tsp oil on each, grill for 20 minutes. After 10 minutes turn side in between and spoon 1 tsp oil on the other side. Continue grilling for the remaining 10 minutes. Serve hot with hari chutney.

Tomato-Kaju Idli

The regular South Indian idlis made more appetizing!

Makes 6 idlis

1 cup suji (rawa)
1½ tbsp oil, 1 cup curd
½ cup water, approx., ½ tsp soda-bicarb
¾ tsp salt

OTHER INGREDIENTS
1 firm tomato - cut into 8 slices
4-5 cashews - split into halves
8-10 curry leaves

1. In a dish put 1½ tbsp oil. Microwave for 1 minute.
2. Add suji. Mix well. Microwave uncovered for 2 minutes.
3. Add salt. Mix well. Allow to cool.
4. Add curd and water. Mix till smooth.
5. Add soda-bicarb. Mix very well till smooth. Keep aside for 10 minutes.
6. Grease 6 small glass katoris or plastic idli boxes. Arrange a slice of tomato, a split cashew half and a curry leaf at the bottom of the katori.
7. Pour 3-4 tbsp mixture into each katori.
8. Arrange katoris in a ring in the microwave and microwave uncovered for 3½ minutes. Do not microwave more even if they appear wet.
9. Let them stand for 5 minutes. They will turn dry. Serve hot with sambhar and chutney.

Dakshini Crispies

Enjoy the South Indian style topping on crisp pieces of bread.

Serves 4

3 bread slices
1 potato
2 tbsp suji (semolina)
½ tsp salt, or to taste
¼ tsp pepper, or to taste
½ onion - very finely chopped
½ tomato - cut into half, deseeded and chopped finely
2 tbsp curry leaves - chopped
½ tsp rai (small brown mustard seeds)

1. Wash potato. Put in a plastic bag and microwave for 3 minutes. Peel and mash coarsely.
2. To the potato, add onion, tomato, curry leaves, salt and pepper. Mix.
3. Add the suji and mix lightly.
4. Spread potato mixture carefully on bread slices, keeping edges neat.
5. Sprinkle some rai over the potato mixture, pressing down gently with finger tips.
6. Keep the bread slices in the microwave oven on the combination mode (convec+grill) and cook for 15 minutes or till the bottom of the slice gets crisp.
7. Cut each toast into 4 triangular or square pieces. Serve with tomato ketchup or mustard sauce.

Paneer Tikka

The universal Indian delight, now made more delicious!

Picture on page 1   *Serves 4*

300 gm paneer- cut into 2" squares of about ¾" thickness
1 large capsicum - cut into 1" pieces or rings
1 onion - cut into 4 pieces
1 tomato - cut into 8 pieces

MARINADE
1 cup dahi - hang in a muslin cloth for 20 minutes
3 tbsp thick malai or thick cream
a few drops of orange colour or a pinch of haldi (turmeric)
1½ tbsp oil, 1 tbsp cornflour
½ tsp amchoor ½ tsp black salt
½ tsp red chilli powder, ¾ tsp salt
1 tbsp tandoori masala or ½ tsp garam masala
1 tbsp ginger-garlic paste

1. Mix all ingredients of the marinade in a bowl. Add paneer. Mix well.
2. Grease wire or grill rack. Arrange paneer on the greased wire rack. After all the paneer pieces are done, put capsicum, onions and tomato together in the left over marinade and mix well to coat the vegetables. Place vegetables also on rack.
3. Set your microwave oven at 200°C using the oven (convection) mode and press start to preheat.
4. Put the tikkas in the hot oven.
5. Re-set the preheated oven again at 200°C for 20 minutes. Cook the tikkas for 15 minutes.
6. Spoon some melted butter on the tikkas and cook further for 5 minutes. Remove from oven. Sprinkle chat masala and lemon juice. Serve hot.

MYTH!

TANDOORI CHICKEN MASALA CONTAINS CHICKEN

No, it is only a blend of masala without any chicken in it. Vegetarians can use it in the recipes without any hesitation.

Soups

Sweet Corn Soup

The all time favourite Chinese soup!

Picture on page 21   *Serves 6-7*

½ tin cream style sweet corn tin (460 gm for full tin- 2½ cups)
¼ cup chopped cabbage
¼ cup grated carrot
1 spring onion - finely chopped, including the greens
1 tsp vinegar
1 tsp red chilli sauce
1 tbsp green chilli sauce
pinch of ajinomoto
¼ tsp pepper
¾ tsp salt, or to taste
2½ tbsp cornflour mixed in ¼ cup water

1. In a deep bowl, mix cream style corn (1¼ cups) with 4 cups water. Microwave for 8 minutes or more till it comes to a boil. Stir once inbetween.
2. Add all other ingredients and microwave again for 5 minutes. Stir once inbetween.
3. Microwave for 1-2 minutes more if the soup is not thick enough. Serve hot with green chillies in vinegar.

Note: The left over cream style corn can be stored in a box in the freezer compartment of the fridge for a month or even more.

Capsicum Soup

A cheesy light green soup.

Serves 4

4 medium sized capsicums - cut into big pieces
2 tomatoes - cut into big pieces
2 cups water
½ cup milk
2 tsp cheese spread
1 tsp salt
½ tsp pepper or to taste
1 tsp butter

1. Microwave capsicum and tomato with 1 cup water in a microproof bowl for 3 minutes.
2. Remove from the microwave, cool.
3. Add 1 cup water. Churn in a mixer to get a smooth puree. Strain puree.
4. To the strained puree add milk, cheese spread, salt, pepper and butter. Microwave for 6 minutes.
5. Pour into individual bowls and serve hot.

Corn Minestrone

A hearty Italian tomato soup with vegetables.

Serves 4-6

½ cup cooked corn kernels (fresh or tinned)
2 mushrooms - sliced very finely
¼ cup finely chopped carrots
1 tbsp finely chopped french beans
¼ cup finely chopped potatoes
2 large tomatoes
1 tbsp butter
2 tbsp chopped onions
5 cups water mixed with a seasoning cube
salt and pepper to taste

GARNISH
2-3 tbsp grated cheese

1. To blanch the tomatoes, put a cross on the stem end of each tomato and place on a microproof plate. Microwave for 2 minutes. Peel the skin and chop them finely.
2. Put butter in a big, deep microproof bowl. Microwave for 30 seconds.
3. Add onions and microwave for 2 minutes.
4. Add corn, mushrooms, carrots, french beans and potatoes. Mix well. Microwave for 5 minutes.
5. Add blanched and chopped tomatoes, pepper and water mixed with a vegetarian seasoning cube. Microwave covered for 8 minutes. Stir once inbetween.
6. Remove from the microwave and mash lightly. Check salt.
7. Serve hot in soup bowls garnished with finely grated cheese.

Indian Curries

Corn Korma Masala

Serves 6-7

8" round, 2½"-3" deep dish with cover

3 tbsp oil
2 medium onions - chopped finely
3-4 moti illaichi (black cardamoms)
2 small tomatoes - chopped finely
1 cup beaten curd
1 tsp red chilli powder, salt to taste , ¼ tsp sugar
¼ tsp haldi (turmeric) powder
1 cup cooked corn kernels (green giant tin)
2 green chillies - deseeded & chopped

MASALA PASTE
1 small piece coconut - grated (¼ cup)
2 tsp khus-khus (poppy seeds)
7-8 cashewnuts or 2 tsp magaz
2-3 green chillies

GARNISHING
a few coriander leaves - chopped finely

1. Grind all the ingredients of the masala paste together with ¼ cup water to a fine paste.
2. In the dish take oil. Add slightly opened cardamoms. Microwave for 2 minute uncovered.
3. Add sugar, red chilli powder, salt & haldi powder. Mix well. Add onions. Microwave for 3 minutes.
4. Add masala paste. Mix well. Add tomatoes. Stir well. Microwave covered for 5 minutes.
5. Add beaten curd. Mix well. Add corn . Add green chillies & garam masala. Mix well. Microwave covered for 7 minutes. Stir once in between.
6. Let stand 3-4 minutes.
7. Sprinkle chopped coriander leaves & serve hot.

Palak Paneer

Spinach and cottage cheese - a wonderful combination!

Serves 4

250 gm paneer - cut into 1" cubes
1 bundle (600 gm) spinach - break the leaves only, discarding the stem
2 tbsp oil
1 tsp cumin seeds (jeera)
½" piece ginger
4-5 flakes of garlic
2 onions - chopped
1 green chilli - chopped
2 tsp coriander powder (dhania powder)
½ tsp garam masala
2 tomatoes - chopped
2 tbsp dry fenugreek leaves (kasoori methi)
1 tbsp butter
½ tsp red chilli powder
¾ tsp salt, ¼ tsp sugar
¼ cup milk

1. In a microproof deep bowl put oil, jeera, ginger, garlic, onions, green chilli, 2 tsp dhania powder and garam masala. Mix well. Microwave for 5 minutes.
2. Add chopped tomatoes and kasoori methi. Mix well. Add washed spinach leaves. Microwave for 8 minutes.
3. Cool spinach. Blend with ½ cup water.
4. Transfer the spinach puree to the same microproof dish. Add 1 tbsp butter, ½ tsp red chilli powder, paneer, ¾ tsp salt, ¼ tsp sugar, ¼ cup milk and ¼ cup water. Mix well.
5. Microwave for 5 minutes. Serve hot.

Ghiya-Channe ki Dal

Gram lentils cooked with bottle gourd and tempered to perfection.

Picture on page 3   *Serves 4*

¾ cup channe ki dal (gram lentils) - washed and soaked for ½ hour
½ small (200 gms) ghiya (bottle gourd) - peeled and chopped
1 tsp salt
½ tsp haldi (turmeric powder)
2 tsp desi ghee or oil
½ tsp red chilli powder

TOMATO-ONION BAGHAR
3 tbsp oil
1 tsp cumin seeds (jeera)
1 onion - finely sliced
1 tomato - finely chopped
2 tbsp chopped coriander
2 green chillies
1 tsp dhania powder
½ tsp garam masala, ½ tsp amchoor
½ tsp red chilli powder

1. Pick, clean and wash dal. Soak for ½ hour.
2. Drain water from dal. Mix dal, ghiya, salt, haldi, desi ghee, red chilli powder and 2 cups water in a deep bowl. Microwave covered for 6 minutes.
3. Stir once inbetween. Remove cover and microwave for 20 minutes or till dal turns soft. Mash lightly. Cover and keep aside.
4. For the baghar, mix oil with jeera in a microproof dish. Microwave for 2 minutes. Add onions and microwave for 4 minutes till golden.
5. Add tomato, coriander and whole green chillies and all the masalas. Microwave for 3 minutes. Pour over the hot cooked dal. Mix gently. Serve hot.

Carrot Kofta Curry

Carrot balls stuffed with raisins in a simple, yet tasty curry.

Serves 4

3 tbsp oil
2 onions - ground to a paste in a mixer
2 tomatoes - pureed in a mixer
2 tsp dhania powder, ¼ tsp haldi
¼ tsp garam masala
¼ tsp red chilli powder

KOFTE
2 carrots - grated
2 bread slices - break into pieces and grind to crumbs in a mixer
1 green chilli - chopped
1 tsp ginger paste, ½ tsp salt
¼ tsp of each - garam masala, amchoor and red chilli powder
2 tbsp yogurt/curd
8-10 kishmish

1. For the gravy, mix onion paste with oil, haldi, dhania powder, garam masala and red chilli powder in a deep microproof dish. Microwave for 8 minutes.
2. Add pureed tomatoes. Microwave for 7 minutes.
3. Add 1½ cups water. Microwave for 6 minutes. Keep aside.
4. For the koftas, mix carrots with all ingredients of the koftas except yogurt and kishmish.
5. Add yogurt. Mix well. Make 8 round balls with 1 kishmish stuffed in each. Place balls on a greased microproof plate in a ring and microwave for 3 minutes.
6. At serving time, place koftas in a serving dish. Pour curry over them. Microwave for 2 minutes and serve.

Water Melon Curry

An unusual thin, spicy curry which is delicious when served with rice.

Picture on facing page   *Serves 4*

**4 cups of tarbooz (water melon) - cut into 1" pieces along with a little white portion
also, and deseeded
4-5 flakes garlic - crushed
½ tsp salt, or to taste
2 tsp lemon juice
2 tbsp oil
½ tsp jeera (cumin seeds)
a pinch of hing (asafoetida)
1 tbsp ginger - cut into thin match sticks
½ tsp dhania (coriander) powder
½ - ¾ tsp red chilli powder
a pinch of haldi (turmeric) powder**

**GARNISH
chopped green chillies and coriander**

1. Puree 1½ cups of water melon cubes (the upper soft pieces) with 4-5 flakes of garlic, salt and lemon juice to get about 1 cup of water melon puree. Leave the remaining firm, lower pieces (with the white portion) as it is. Keep aside.
2. Put oil, jeera, hing, ginger, coriander powder, red chilli powder and haldi in a microproof dish. Mix well. Microwave for 2 minutes.
3. Add the remaining water melon pieces or cubes and stir to mix.
4. Add the prepared puree and microwave for 5 minutes. Remove from microwave.
5. Garnish with green chillies and green coriander. Serve hot with boiled rice.

Makai-Mirch Salan

Baby corn and green chillies in a red gravy flavoured with cumin and mustard seeds.

Serves 4-5

5-6 big acchari hari mirch, 1 tbsp vinegar
200 gm babycorns - keep whole if small or cut into 2 pieces if big
3 tbsp oil
1 tsp jeera (cumin seeds)
½ tsp mustard seeds (rai)
a few curry leaves
2 onions - chopped finely
2 tsp coriander (dhania) powder
1 tsp salt, ¼ tsp red chilli powder
½ tsp dry mango powder (amchoor)
¼ tsp garam masala
1½ cups readymade tomato puree
1 tsp ginger paste
3 tbsp roasted peanuts
1 cup water, ¾ cup milk

1. Slit the mirch and remove seeds. Sprinkle ½ tsp salt and 1 tbsp vinegar. Rub well and keep aside for 15 minutes. Wash and pat dry on a kitchen towel.
2. Churn peanuts with ¼ cup milk in a mixer to get a paste. Keep aside.
3. In a microproof dish put oil, jeera, rai, curry leaves, chopped onions, dhania powder, salt, red chilli powder, amchoor and garam masala. Mix well. Microwave for 8 minutes.
4. Add mirchi, baby corns, redymade tomato puree and ginger paste. Microwave for 6 minutes.
5. Add prepared peanut paste and 1 cup water. Mix well. Microwave for 5 minutes. Stir well.
6. Add ½ cup milk. Microwave for 1 minute. Serve hot.

◄ *Subz Pullao: Recipe on page 70*

Mixed Veggie Curry

Seasonal vegetables in a red tomato based gravy flavoured with cloves and cardamoms.

Serves 4

¼ of a small cauliflower - cut into 8 small ½" florets
1 carrot - cut into thin round slices
10 french beans - cut into ½" pieces
1 capsicum - cut into ½" cubes
50 gm paneer - cut into ½" cubes
¾ cup ready made tomato puree
1½ tsp salt, or to taste
1½ cups milk (cold)

GRIND TO A PASTE
2 onions, 2 tbsp ghee or oil
½ " piece ginger, 3-4 flakes garlic
2 laung (cloves)
seeds of 1 chhoti illaichi
1 tsp dhania powder
¾ tsp jeera - crushed to a powder
½ tsp garam masala powder
¼-½ tsp red chilli powder

1. Cut all the vegetables into ½" pieces. Wash cauliflower, carrots and beans. Microwave together for 3 minutes in a plastic bag or a covered dish. Keep aside.
2. Grind together all ingredients of the paste. Put onion paste in the dish. Microwave uncovered for 8 minutes.
3. Add tomato puree, salt, all microwaved vegetables and capsicum. Mix well.
4. Microwave for 4 minutes.
5. Add paneer and milk. Mix well. Keep aside till serving time.
6. To serve, microwave for 3 minutes.

Khumb Matar Miloni

Mushroom and peas in a tomato - yogurt gravy.

Serves 4

1 packet (200 gm) mushrooms (khumb)
1 cup peas (shelled)
2 tbsp oil, 1 tsp ginger-garlic paste
1 tbsp fenugreek leaves (kasoori methi)

PASTE - 1
2 onions, 2 laung (cloves)
2 green cardamoms (chhoti illaichi)
1 tsp saunf (fennel)
¼ tsp turmeric powder, 3 tbsp oil

PASTE - 2
3 tomatoes - cut into 4 pieces
½ cup yogurt (dahi)
1¼ tsp salt, ½ tsp garam masala
½ tsp degi mirch or red chilli powder

1. Cut each mushroom into 4 pieces.
2. Put 2 tbsp oil, ginger- garlic paste and mushrooms in a microproof dish. Mix and spread them in the dish. Microwave for 3 minutes. Remove mushrooms from the dish and keep aside.
3. Grind all the ingredients of paste-1 in a mixer to a smooth paste.
4. Grind all the ingredients of paste-2 in a mixer to a smooth paste.
5. For the masala, put the paste-1 of onions in the same microproof dish and microwave for 7 minutes.
6. Add paste-2 of tomatoes and kasoori methi. Mix and microwave for 7 minutes.
7. Add 2 cups water and peas. Microwave for 6 minutes.
8. Add the mushrooms. Microwave for 2 minutes. Serve hot.

Special Sambar

The pulse is blended in a mixer to get a smooth and creamy sambhar.

Serves 4

½ cup arhar dal (red gram dal)
100 gm pumpkin or 2 small brinjals or any other vegetable of your choice -
chopped (1 cup)
lemon sized ball of imli (tamarind)
1½ tsp salt or to taste
¼ tsp hing powder (asafoetida)
2 tbsp sambhar powder
1 tbsp oil
1 onion - sliced
½ tsp sarson (mustard seeds)
¼ cup curry leaves
tiny piece of gur (jaggery) - optional

1. Put dal in a microproof bowl. Add 1 cup water and microwave covered for 5 minutes. Remove the cover and microwave for 5 more minutes or till dal turns soft. Cool. Add ½ cup water. Mix. Blend in a mixer to a puree.
2. Microwave imli in ½ cup water for 2 minutes. Extract the juice. Add 1 more cup water to the left over imli and mash well. Extract more juice. Keep imli juice aside.
3. Put oil, curry leaves, sarson, sambhar powder and onions in a deep microproof bowl. Mix well. Microwave for 5 minutes.
4. Add the chopped vegetables, salt, pureed dal and imli paani. Cover and microwave for 6 minutes.
5. Add 2 cups water and microwave for 8 minutes. Serve hot.

Khoya Matar

Peas combine with crumbly dried whole milk to give a rich dish.

Serves 4

200 gms khoya - mashed roughly or crumbled
2 cups shelled peas
4 tbsp oil or desi ghee
¾ cup ready made tomato puree
1 tsp red chilli powder
1 tsp jeera (cumin) powder
¾ tsp garam masala powder
6-8 cashewnuts - split into 2 pieces
1 tsp salt, or to taste

GRIND TOGETHER (ONION PASTE)
2 onions
2 dry, red chillies
1" piece ginger

1. In a dish, mix oil and onion paste. Microwave for 8 minutes.
2. Add tomato puree, garam masala, red chilli powder, jeera powder, peas and ¼ cup water. Mix well.
3. Microwave for 4 minutes.
4. Add salt, khoya and ½ cup water. Mix gently so as not to mash the khoya. Sprinkle cashew halves.
5. Microwave for 3 minutes. Serve hot.

Paneer Pista Haryali

You can add anything else also, instead of paneer in this rich green gravy.

Serves 4

200 gm paneer - cut into 1" squares
2 medium sized onions - cut into 4 pieces
¼ cup pistas (pistachio nuts) with the hard cover on - remove hard cover
½ cup milk

GRIND TOGETHER TO A PASTE
1 green chilli - roughly chopped
¼ cup chopped fresh coriander
1" ginger piece and 4-5 flakes garlic
1 tbsp dhania powder (ground coriander)
½ tsp white pepper powder
¾ tsp salt, or to taste
4 tbsp oil

1. Peel and cut each onion into 4 pieces. Put onion pieces and pistas in 1 cup water in a microproof dish and microwave covered for 6 minutes. Cool slightly. Slip the skin of pistas.
2. Grind boiled onion pieces and the pistas along with the water, and with all the other ingredients written under paste to a fine green paste.
3. Put the prepared paste in a microproof dish and microwave for 5 minutes.
4. Add ½ cup water, a small pinch of sugar and paneer and microwave for 2 minutes. Keep aside till serving time.
5. At serving time, add ½ cup milk or slightly more to get a thick gravy. Microwave for 2 minutes. Serve hot.

Bharwan Tamatar

Tomato stuffed with crunchy rice and put in a gravy.

Serves 4

6 small firm tomatoes, 2 tbsp oil
2 tbsp tomato ketchup
FILLING
1½ cups cooked rice
1 tbsp roasted peanuts - roughly crushed
¼ cup chopped coriander
2 tbsp grated cheese
2 green chillies - deseeded and chopped
1 tsp chaat masala, salt to taste
½ tsp garam masala
GRAVY
2 big onions, 1" piece ginger
½ tsp (turmeric powder) haldi
1 tsp dhania (coriander) powder
½ tsp chilli powder, ¾ tsp salt
½ tsp garam masala, ¼ tsp amchoor

1. Slice a small piece from the top of each tomato. Scoop out carefully.
2. Rub some salt inside the tomatoes and keep them upside down.
3. Mix all ingredients of the filling. Do not mash. Mix gently.
4. Fill scooped tomatoes with the filling. Press well.
5. Grind all ingredients of gravy along with the scooped out portion of the tomatoes, together in a mixer.
6. Put oil and onion-tomato paste in a microproof bowl. Microwave for 11 minutes or more, till paste turns dry.
7. Add 1½ cups water and tomato ketchup. Mix well. Microwave for 6 minutes.
8. Arrange stuffed tomatoes on the gravy. Keep aside till serving time.
9. To serve, microwave for 3 minutes or till tomatoes turn soft.

Aloo Matar Curry

Serves 4-5

6"-7" round, 4"-5" deep dish

1 cup shelled peas (matar)
1 potato - cut into ½" cubes (small even cubes)
2 medium onions - minced (chopped very finely)
2-3 flakes garlic - chopped finely
½" piece ginger - chopped finely
3 tbsp oil
¼ tsp haldi
½-1 tsp red chilli powder
2 tsp dhania powder
½ tsp garam masala powder
2 large tomatoes - ground to a puree
1 tsp salt
1 tbsp coriander leaves - chopped

1. In a deep dish, microwave uncovered oil, onion, ginger & garlic for 4 minutes.
2. Add haldi powder, dhania powder, garam masala powder, red chilli powder. Mix well.
3. Add fresh tomato puree. Mix well. Microwave uncovered 6 minutes. Stir once in between.
4. Add shelled peas, potatoes and 1 cup water. Mix well.
5. Microwave covered 5-7 minutes or till potatoes become soft.
6. Add salt and coriander leaves.
7. Microwave 1 minute.
8. Let it stand for 2-3 minutes. Serve hot.

Paneer Makhani

Paneer in a red cashew based makhani gravy flavoured with fenugreek.

Serves 4-5   *Picture on page 2*

300 gm paneer - cut into cubes
5 large (500 gm) tomatoes - chopped roughly
1" piece ginger - chopped
2 tbsp butter/ghee and 2 tbsp oil
seeds of 2 green illaichi (cardamoms) - crushed
½ tsp sugar, 1 tsp salt or to taste
½ tsp garam masala
½ tsp degi mirch or red chilli powder
1 tsp tomato ketchup
4 tbsp cashewnuts or magaz - soaked in ¼ cup water and ground to a paste
2 tsp kasoori methi (dried fenugreek leaves)
1 cup milk, approx.
3-4 tbsp cream

1. Microwave tomatoes and ginger in a deep dish with ½ cup water for 5 minutes.
2. Blend tomatoes and ginger to a puree in a mixer.
3. Microwave butter/ghee and oil for 2 minutes. Add illaichi powder. Mix. Add salt, sugar, red chilli powder and garam masala. Mix. Add fresh tomato puree and tomato ketchup. Mix very well. Microwave for 8 minutes. Stir once in between.
4. Add cashewnut or magaz paste and kasoori methi. Mix well. Add ½ cup water. Microwave for 3 minutes.
5. Add paneer and mix well. Add enough milk to get a thick red gravy. Mix well and microwave for 3 minutes.
6. Add cream. Sprinkle little kasoori methi on top and serve hot.

Achaari Khumb Mirch

Mushrooms and capsicums in a pickle flavoured masala.

Serves 4

200 gms (1 packet) fresh mushrooms - each cut into 4 pieces
2 capsicums - cut into ¼" pieces
2 tbsp oil
2 onions - cut into rings and separated
1 tsp dhania powder
¼ tsp haldi (turmeric)
¼ tsp amchoor
½ tsp garam masala
½ tsp red chilli powder
1" piece ginger - cut into match sticks
1 tsp salt
1½ tbsp lemon juice, or to taste

ACHARI SPICES (½ TSP EACH)
½ tsp saunf (fennel)
½ tsp jeera (cumin seeds)
½ tsp rai (brown mustard seeds)
½ tsp kalaunji (nigella or onion seeds)

1. In a microproof flat dish, put oil, onion, dhania powder, haldi, amchoor, garam masala and red chilli powder. Add all the achari spices also and mix well. Microwave for 7 minutes.
2. Add ginger, mushrooms, salt and lemon juice. Mix very well and spread them out in the dish. Microwave for 8 minutes. Stir once in-between.
3. Add capsicum and mix. Microwave for 3 minutes and serve.

Anjeeri Gobhi

Cauliflower cooked with a hint of sweetness in a yogurt and dry figs paste.

Picture on cover   *Serves 4-6*

(1 big) ½ kg cauliflower (gobhi) - cut into medium size florets with long stalks
1 tsp jeera (cumin seeds)
2 onions - chopped
¾" piece ginger- chopped
¼ tsp turmeric (haldi)
2 green chillies
1 tomato - chopped

ANJEER PASTE
8 small anjeers (figs) - chopped
¾ cup dahi (yogurt)
½ tsp garam masala
½ tsp red chilli powder
1½ tsp salt

1. Break the cauliflower into medium florets, keeping the stalk intact.
2. Churn all the ingredients given under anjeer paste in a mixer till smooth.
3. In a microproof dish put 4 tbsp oil, jeera, chopped onions and ginger. Add haldi. Mix. Microwave for 9 minutes.
4. Add the prepared anjeer paste. Mix well. Add cauliflower and mix very well. Mix in whole green chillies and chopped tomato. Cover and microwave for 10 minutes or more till the cauliflower gets cooked.

Paneer Hara Pyaz

Green spring onions with cottage cheese in masala.

Serves 4

250 gm paneer- cut into 1" cubes
150 gm hare pyaz (spring onions)
1 green chilli - deseeded and chopped
3 tbsp oil
6-8 flakes garlic - crushed
¼ tsp turmeric powder (haldi)
2 tsp coriander (dhania) powder
¾ cup readymade tomato puree
1 tbsp tomato ketchup
3 laung (cloves) - crushed
½ tsp red chilli powder
½ tsp garam masala
¾ tsp salt
4 tbsp cream or well beaten thin malai

1. Cut white of spring onions into rings, greens into ½" diagonal pieces.
2. Put oil, garlic, white of onion, haldi and dhania powder in a microproof dish. Microwave for 4 minutes.
3. Add tomato puree, tomato ketchup, laung, red chilli powder, garam masala and salt. Mix well. Microwave for 4 minutes.
4. Add ½ cup water, paneer, green chillies, cream and about 1 cup of greens of spring onions. Mix well. Microwave for 2 minutes. Check salt and add more if required. Mix and serve hot.

Bharwan Baingan

Brinjals stuffed with a crunchy sesame filling.

Serves 4

8 (300 gm) small brinjals (baingans)
3 tbsp oil
½ tsp cumin seeds (jeera)
1 onion - grated
1½ tsp ginger-garlic paste
¼ tsp each of - sugar, salt, garam masala and red chilli powder
1 tsp full tamarind (imli)

STUFFING (MIX TOGETHER)
2 tbsp roasted peanuts - crushed roughly
2 tsp sesame seeds (til)
1 tsp salt, ½ tsp amchoor,
½ tsp haldi, ½ tsp sugar
½ tsp red chilli pd, ½ tsp garam masala
2 tsp dhania powder
2 tsp oil

1. Put imli with ½ cup water in a small bowl. Microwave for 1 minute. Let it cool. Mash and extract juice and keep aside

2. Wash and slit brinjals, making cross cuts, a little more than half way.

3. Mix all ingredients of the stuffing nicely. Fill the paste in the baingans.

4. Arrange brinjals in a dish. Pour 2 tbsp oil on them. Microwave covered for 8 minutes. Remove from dish and keep aside.

5. In the same dish put 1 tbsp oil, jeera, onion and ginger-garlic paste. Mix well and microwave for 4 min.

6. Add tamarind juice, ¼ tsp of sugar, salt, garam masala and red chilli powder. Mix well. Add cooked brinjals and mix gently for the masala to coat. Microwave covered for 2 minutes. Serve hot.

Dal Maharani

Split and dehusked black lentils cooked till each grain stands out separately.

Serves 4

1 cup dhuli urad dal (split black beans) - soaked for 1 hour
1 onion - sliced
1" piece ginger - grated
3 tbsp oil
1¼ tsp salt
½ tsp turmeric powder (haldi)
½ tsp red chilli powder
¼ tsp amchoor
¼ tsp coriander (dhania) powder

1. Clean and wash dal. Soak in water for 1 hour.
2. Keep onion and ginger in a microproof dish. Sprinkle oil on it. Mix. Add salt, haldi, chilli powder, amchoor and dhania powder. Microwave for 6 minutes.
3. Drain the dal and add dal to the onions. Add 2 cups water. Mix well. Microwave covered for 20 minutes. Stir once after 8 minutes in-between.
4. After it is ready, let it stand for 3-4 minutes till it turns soft. Sprinkle chopped coriander and mix gently with a fork.

Mili-Juli-Subzi

Mixed vegetables flavoured with cardamoms.

Picture on facing page   *Serves 4*

1 big potato
200 gm (1 packet of 15- 20 pieces) baby cabbage (brussel sprouts) - trim the stalk
end or use ½ of a small cabbage - cut into 1" pieces
100 gms baby corns (7-8) - keep whole
½ cup peas (matar)
1 carrot - cut into ¼" pieces (½ cup)
8-10 french beans - cut into ½" pieces
15 cherry tomatoes or 2 regular tomatoes - cut into 4, remove pulp

ONION PASTE (GRIND TOGETHER)
1 onion, 2 cloves (laung)
seeds of 2 green cardamoms (illaichi)

TOMATO PASTE (GRIND TOGETHER)
2 tomatoes
¼ cup curd
¼ tsp haldi, 1 tsp salt, ½ tsp chilli pd.
½ tsp garam masala, ½ tsp degi mirch

1. Peel potato and make balls with the help of a melon scooper.
2. Put 1 cup of water, 2 tsp salt, potato balls in a deep bowl and microwave for 5 minutes.
3. To the same water add cabbage, baby corns, peas, carrots and french beans. Microwave covered for 2 minutes. Strain.
4. Put 3 tbsp oil and onion paste in a microproof bowl. Microwave for 5 minutes.
5. Add tomato paste. Mix. Microwave for 7 minutes.
6. Add ½ cup water and vegetables. Mix well. Microwave covered for 3 minutes. Serve hot.

Crispy Achaari Mirch

Peppers filled with pickle masala rice and grilled with a semolina coating till crisp.

Serves 6

125 gms (6) big, fat green chillies (achari hari mirch) or 3 small capsicums
FILLING
1½ cups boiled rice, ¼ cup vinegar
½ tsp brown mustard seeds (rai)
½ tsp jeera (cumin seeds), ½ tsp saunf (fennel seeds)
1 onion - chopped
¼ tsp haldi (turmeric powder)
2 tsp of any achaar ka masala (preferably use aam ka achaar)
1 tomato - chopped
½ tsp salt, 1 tsp tomato ketchup
COATING
2 tbsp maida (flour), 4 tbsp suji (semolina)
¼ tsp salt
¼ tsp garlic paste

1. Slit the chillies and remove the seeds. Pour vinegar on them and sprinkle ¼ tsp salt on them. Mix. Keep aside.
2. In a microproof dish put 1 tbsp oil, jeera, rai, saunf, chopped onion, and haldi. Mix well. Microwave for 5 minutes.
3. Add boiled rice, aam ke aachar ka masala, ½ tsp salt, chopped tomato and tomato ketchup. Mix well.
4. Fill each mirchi with the filling. Fill as much as the mirchi can take.
5. Mix ingredients of coating in a plate.
6. Put 2-3 tbsp oil in a bowl. Dip the sides of the mirchi in the oil and then immediately roll over the coating spread in the plate. Coat all the sides of the mirchi with the coating mixture nicely.
7. Grill for 12-15 minutes or till golden. Serve hot.

◁ *Veggie Thai Red Curry: Recipe on page 78*

Achaari Bhindi

Crispy fried lady's fingers with pickle spices.

Serves 4

500 gm bhindi (lady's finger)
1 tsp ginger paste
½ tsp red chilli powder
1 tsp dhania powder
½ tsp amchoor, ½ tsp garam masala
¾ tsp salt, or to taste
2 big tomatoes - chopped
1 tsp lemon juice

ACHAARI SPICES
a pinch of hing (asafoetida)
1 tsp saunf (fennel), ½ tsp rai (mustard seeds)
½ tsp kalonji (onion seeds)

1. Wash bhindi and wipe dry. Cut the tip of the head of each bhindi, leaving the pointed end as it is. Now cut the bhindi vertically from the middle making 2 smaller pieces from each bhindi.
2. Keep bhindi in a dish. Sprinkle 2 tbsp oil on it. Mix well. Put them in the oven on combination mode (micro+grill) for 15 minutes or till cooked and crisp. Keep aside.
3. In the separate small dish put 2 tbsp oil and achari spices. Microwave for 3 minutes.
4. To the bhindi, add achari spices, dry masala powders, salt, ginger paste, tomatoes and lemon juice. Mix very well. Microwave for 4 minutes.

Baingan ka Bharta

Serves 3-4

1 medium brinjal of round variety (350 gm)
2 onions - chopped finely
½ cup ready-made tomato puree
1 tomato - chopped
½" piece ginger - chopped finely
1 green chilli - chopped
2 tsp dhania (coriander) powder
½ tsp garam masala
½ tsp degi mirch or red chilli powder
1 tsp salt

1. Place brinjal in a micr proof flat dish. Microwave for 5 minutes. Let it cool down.
2. Cut brinjal into half and scoop out the pulp. Mash the pulp with a fork and keep pulp aside.
3. In the same dish, put oil, onions, ginger, green chilli, dhania powder, garam masala, degi mirch and microwave for 7 minutes.
4. Add brinjal pulp and cook on combination mode (micro + grill) for 10 minutes.
5. Add chopped tomato and tomato puree and 1 tsp salt. Mix well. Microwave for 6 minutes. Serve hot.

Grilled Besani Subzi

Gramflour and carom seeds on top of mixed vegetables give a fragrant roasted flavour when grilled.

Serves 4

2 carrots - cut into thin round slices
2 capsicums - sliced into thin fingers
75 gm paneer - cut into thin fingers (¾ cup)
3 tbsp oil
½ tsp ajwain (carom seeds)
3 tbsp besan (gramflour)
1 tsp lemon juice
¼ tsp red chilli powder
¼ tsp dhania powder
¼ tsp haldi
2 tsp channa masala
2 tsp amchoor
1 tbsp milk
1 tsp salt
1 tomato - deseeded and cut into thin fingers

1. Microwave sliced carrots with ¼ cup water in a microproof dish for 3 minutes.
2. In another microproof dish put oil, ajwain, besan, lemon juice, red chilli powder, dhania powder, haldi, channa masala and amchoor. Mix and microwave for 2 minutes.
3. Add carrot, capsicum, paneer, milk and salt.
4. Grill in the oven for 16 minutes. After 8 minutes, add deseeded tomatoes and mix gently with a fork and grill for the remaining 8 minutes. Serve hot.

Kadhai Paneer

Serves 4

6" round, 3" deep dish with cover

200 gms paneer - cut into thin fingers
3 tbsp oil, 5-6 flakes garlic - crushed
½ cup ready made tomato puree
1 tsp salt
½ tsp sugar
¾ tsp red chilli powder (to taste)
1 tsp dhania powder
½ tsp garam masala
1 capsicum - cut into thin long strips

1. In a dish add oil and garlic. Microwave uncovered 2 minutes.
2. Add tomato puree. Add salt, sugar, red chilli powderd, dhania & garam masala. Mix well. Add capsicum. Mix. Microwave uncovered for 3 minutes.
3. Add paneer. Mix well. Keep aside. At serving time, microwave covered for 2 minutes. Serve hot in a small copper kadhai.

Stir Fried Baby Corns

Serves 3-4

250 gm (6) baby corns
1 capsicum - cut into finger shaped pieces
1 onion - sliced
1 small tomato - cut into long pieces
seeds of 2 chhoti illaichi (green cardamom) - crushed to a rough powder
¼ tsp ajwain - crushed to a rough powder
¼ tsp haldi
¼ tsp garam masala
¼ tsp red chilli powder
½ - ¾ tsp salt
1 tbsp oil

1. Cut each baby corn into 2 pieces. Cut each piece into two lengthwise. Each baby corn gives 4 finger shaped pieces.
2. Microwave 1 tbsp oil, ajwain, onions and babycorn together for 3 minutes.
3. Add haldi, red chilli powder, garam masala and salt. Mix well.
4. Add capsicum strips, tomato pieces and chhoti illaichi. Microwave for 3 minutes.
5. Let it stand for 2 minutes. Serve hot.

Zayekedar Arbi

Serves 3-4

8" round, 1-2" high dish

10 medium sized pieces of arbi (400 gm) - peeled & halved lengthways
1" piece ginger - grated finely
4-5 flakes garlic - chopped & crushed
1-2 green chillies - chopped very finely
¾ tsp salt
juice of ½ lemon
1 tsp ajwain - crushed roughly

MASALA
6 tbsp thick curd
1 tsp besan (gram flour)
1 tbsp fresh coriander chopped
1 tbsp (poodina) mint leaves - chopped
2 tsp oil
½ tsp salt, ½ tsp red chilli powder, ½ tsp garam masala, ½ tsp amchoor

1. Choose even sized arbi & it should not be too thick. Peel, slit into half length ways. If the arbi is thick, cut lengthways into 3 pieces. Rub 2 tsp salt on it nicely and keep aside for 10 minutes or more. Wash well. Strain. Wipe dry.
2. Place arbi in a flat dish. Sprinkle all the ingredients given under the arbi on it. Rub them well over the arbi.
3. Microwave 2 minutes uncovered. Turn pieces over with tongs or spoon. Again microwave 2 minutes uncovered.
4. Beat curd with a spoon in a small bowl. Add all the other ingredients of the masala and mix well.
5. Sprinkle the dahi mix on the arbi and mix well. Microwave covered for 6 minutes.
6. Let it stand for 2 minutes. Serve sprinkled with a little lemon juice.

Saunf ke Karele

Serves 4-5

7-8 " round, 1-2" high dish (flat dish)

½ kg karelas (bitter gourd) - peeled, slit, seeds removed & rubbed with salt & kept
aside for 2-3 hours
4 onions - chopped
½" piece ginger - chopped finely
2 green chillies - chopped finely
3 tbsp oil
2 tsp moti saunf (big fennel seeds)

DRY MASALA
¼ tsp haldi, ½ tsp salt
1 tsp amchoor (dried mango powder)
½ tsp red chilli powder, ½ tsp garam masala

1. Peel karelas. Give a cut in the centre. Carefully remove all the seeds. Rub salt inside and over the karelas. Keep aside for 2-3 hours or more. You could do this part of the work in the morning and put away the karelas in the fridge, if they have to be prepared for dinner.
2. Wash kerelas well to remove bitterness. Microwave uncovered for 8 minutes on a plate or a flat dish.
3. In a flat dish, microwave oil for 3 minutes.
4. Add saunf. Mix well. Add onions, ginger and green chillies. Sprinkle all the ingredients given under dry masala. Mix very well. Microwave for 7 minutes. Stir once in between.
5. Fill the filling in the karelas. Close the sides with the help of a wooden tooth pick. Arrange in the same dish, side by side. Sprinkle 1 tbsp oil over the karelas.
6. Cover and microwave for 4 minutes. Serve.

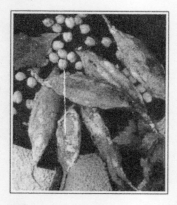

Rice

Steamed Rice

Rice prepared in the microwave should not be served immediately as it tastes uncooked if done so. Microwaved rice is wonderful, each grain is soft and separate, if served after 10 minutes, once the microwave is shut off.

Serves 2

1 cup basmati rice - washed and soaked for ½ hour
½ tsp salt
1 tsp lemon juice
2 cups water

1. Drain the soaked rice. Put in a broad, shallow microproof dish (a pie dish).
2. Add salt, lemon juice and 2 cups water. Mix well.
3. Microwave covered for 11 minutes. Serve after 10 minutes.

Carrot Pepper Rice

Serves 2-3

1 cup rice - soaked for 15-20 minutes
3 tbsp oil, 1 onion - sliced
1 capsicum and 1 carrot - chopped
1 tsp salt, ½ tsp freshly crushed pepper
½ tsp soya sauce

1. Mix oil, onion, capsicum, carrot in a big microproof dish and microwave for 3 minutes.
2. Add rice, 2 cups water, salt, pepper and soya sauce. Microwave covered for 13 minutes. Stir once in between. Sprinkle pepper. Serve after 5 minutes.

Matar waale Chaawal

Serves 4

9-10" round, 2-3 " high dish

1 cup basmati rice - soaked for 1 hour
1 cup shelled peas
½" piece ginger - grated
1 large onion- sliced finely
1½ tsp salt
¼ tsp red chilli powder
¼ tsp garam masala
2-3 laung (cloves)
2 green chillies
2 tbsp chopped coriander
1 firm tomato - cut into strips & pulp removed
3 tbsp oil

1. Microwave oil in a large dish for 2 minutes.
2. Add peas, onions, ginger, salt, chilli powder, garam masala and laung. Microwave for 3 minutes.
3. Drain the rice and add to it. Add 2 cups water, whole green chillies, coriander leaves and tomato strips. Mix well.
4. Microwave covered for 11 minutes. Stir once after 5 minutes.
5. Let it stand for 2 minutes. Fluff it up with a fork to separate the grains. Serve hot.

Subz Pullao

The spice bag added to rice and the vegetables, makes it very aromatic.

Picture on page 40   *Serves 3-4*

1 cup basmati rice - washed and soaked
5 tbsp oil
1 tsp ginger paste, ½ tsp garlic paste
¼ tsp haldi, ½ tsp red chilli powder
1½ tsp salt or to taste

SABOOT MASALA OR SPICE BAG (*crush together and tie in a piece of muslin cloth*)
10 saboot kali mirch (pepper corns)
2 tsp saunf (fennel seeds)
3-4 chhoti illaichi (green cardamom)
3-4 moti illaichi (black cardamom)
4 laung (cloves)
2 sticks dalchini (cinnamon)

VEGETABLES
1 potato - cut into ½" pieces
½ of a small cauliflower - cut into florets
2 carrots - cut into ½" pieces
1 cup green peas
1 tomato - cut into 8 pieces
2-3 green chillies - cut into thin strips
1 tbsp mint leaves, 1 tsp lemon juice

1. In a broad microproof dish, put oil, ginger, garlic, cauliflower, potato, carrots and peas. Microwave for 3 minutes.
2. Drain the soaked rice. Add rice, 2 cups water, haldi, red chilli pd and salt. Add the spice bag. Microwave covered for 6 minutes.
3. Add tomatoes, mint, coriander, green chillies and lemon juice. Stir gently with a fork. Cover and microwave for 7 minutes. Wait for 5 minutes. Fluff with a fork. Remove spice bag. Serve.

Corn in Soya Sauce

Perfectly cooked corn in the microwave put in a sauce flavoured predominantly with soya sauce.

Serves 2

1 corn on the cob with the green husk (saboot bhutta with chilka)
5-6 small spring onions
½ cup cabbage cut into 1" pieces
1 vegetable seasoning cube - crushed
1 green chilli - chopped
2 tbsp oil
¼ tsp pepper
1 tsp mustard paste
1½ tsp soya sauce
1 tbsp cornflour dissolved in ¾ cup water and ¼ cup milk

1. Push down the husk of the corn a little to open slightly and wash the corn on the cob. Pull up the husk back to cover corn and microwave the full corn for 3 minutes. Remove husk from the cooked corn and scrape out the corn niblets from the corn cob with the help of a knife. Keep aside.

2. Let white portion of the spring onion remain as it is and cut the green portion into 1" pieces.

3. In a microproof dish mix white bulbs of spring onions, cabbage pieces, crushed seasoning cube, chopped green chilli, oil, pepper, mustard paste and soya sauce. Microwave uncovered for 2 minutes.

4. Add cornflour paste. Mix well. Microwave uncovered for 3 minutes or till sauce boils and thickens slightly. Stir once after 2 minutes. Add greens of spring onions.

5. Keep aside covered for 2-3 minutes. Mix well before serving. Serve hot.

Glass Noodles with Sesame Paste

Serves 6

100 gms glass noodles or rice seviyaan
2 tbsp oil
3 spring onions - cut into rings, till the greens, keep white separate

SESAME PASTE (GRIND ALL TOGETHER)
3 tbsp sesame seeds (til) - soak for 10 minutes in 5 tbsp hot milk and 2 tbsp water
½ tsp red chilli powder or to taste
¾ tsp salt
4 flakes garlic - finely chopped
1½ tbsp soya sauce, ½ tsp sugar

1. Cut white spring onion into rings till the greens.
2. In a deep bowl microwave 3 cups water with 1 tsp salt and 1 tsp oil for 8 minutes. Add noodles to hot water. Cover and keep aside for 5 minutes in hot water. Drain noodles.
3. Wash with cold water several times. Strain. Leave them in the strainer for 15-20 minutes, turning them upside down, once after about 10 minutes to ensure complete drying. Apply 1 tsp oil on the noodles and spread on a large tray. Dry the noodles under a fan for 15-20 minutes. Keep aside till further use.
4. Grind all ingredients of sesame paste to a smooth paste.
5. Mix oil and white of spring onions in a microproof dish and microwave for 3 minutes.
6. Add prepared sesame mixture, mix well and microwave for 1 minute.
7. Add noodles, mix well. Add spring onion greens. Mix.
8. Microwave for 1 minute at serving time.

Honey Chilli Veggies

Sweet and spicy mixed vegetables with Chinese sauces.

Picture on facing page   *Serves 4*

1 large carrot
8-10 mushrooms - keep whole
8-9 baby corns - keep whole if small and divide into two lengthwise, if thick
1½ cups cauliflower or broccoli - cut into small, flat florets
1 onion - cut into 8 pieces
1 capsicum - cut into ½" cubes
4 tbsp oil
2-3 dry, red chillies - broken into bits and deseeded
15 flakes garlic - crushed
¾ tsp salt and ¼ tsp pepper, or to taste
a pinch ajinomoto (optional)
1½ tbsp vinegar, 1 tsp soya sauce
2½ tbsp tomato ketchup
2-3 tsp red chilli sauce
3-4 tsp honey, according to taste
3 tbsp cornflour dissolved in ½ cup water alongwith 1 seasoning cube

1. Dissolve cornflour in ½ cup water. Add seasoning cube and keep aside.
2. Put oil, broken red chillies, garlic, baby corns, mushrooms, carrots, cauliflower and onion in a microproof dish. Mix well. Microwave for 5 minutes.
3. Add pepper, salt, ajinomoto, chilli sauce, tomato sauce, soya sauce, honey, and vinegar. Mix and microwave for 1 minute.
4. Add capsicum and dissolved cornflour and mix. Microwave for 3 minutes or till the vegetables are crisp-tender and the sauce coats the veggies. Mix well before serving. Serve hot with rice or noodles.

Broccoli in Butter Sauce

Broccoli in the new white Chinese sauce prepared from butter and milk and thickened with flour.

Serves 4   *Picture on opposite page*

250 gm (1 medium head) broccoli
1 tsp salt, 1 tsp sugar

SAUCE
1 veg seasoning cube
3 tbsp butter
1 onion - sliced
1 tbsp crushed garlic (15 flakes)
1 tbsp chopped coriander
3 tbsp flour (maida)
1 cup milk
2 tsp mustard paste
½ tsp pepper, ¾ tsp salt, or to taste
1 cup thin cream

1. Cut broccoli into medium sized florets with long stalks.
2. Put 1 cup water in a microproof bowl. Add 1 tsp salt and 1 tsp sugar and mix. Add broccoli to it and mix well. Microwave covered for 3 minutes. Drain. Refresh in cold water. Wipe dry broccoli with a clean kitchen towel.
3. Put 3 tbsp butter in a microproof dish and microwave for 30 seconds. Add sliced onion, crushed garlic and microwave for 5 minutes.
4. Add broccoli, coriander, crushed seasoning cube and maida. Mix and microwave for 1 minute.
5. Add milk, ¾ cup water, mustard paste, pepper and salt. Mix and microwave for 6 minutes or till sauce thickens. Stir once in between. Remove.
6. Add cream. Mix. Keep aside till serving time. At serving time, microwave for 2 minutes.

Veggie Thai Red Curry

Mixed vegetables in a lemon flavoured, spicy red curry prepared from coconut milk.

Picture on page 58   *Serves 4-6*

RED CURRY PASTE
4-5 dry, Kashmiri red chillies - soaked in ½ cup warm water for 10 minutes
½ onion - chopped
8-10 flakes garlic - peeled
1½" piece ginger - chopped
1 stalk lemon grass or rind of 1 lemon
1½ tsp coriander seeds (dhania saboot)
1 tsp cumin seeds (jeera)
6 peppercorns (saboot kali mirch)
1 tsp salt, 1 tbsp vinegar

VEGETABLES
7-8 baby corns - slit lengthwise
2 small brinjals - peeled and diced
1 small broccoli or ½ cauliflower - cut into small florets
7-8 mushrooms - sliced

OTHER INGREDIENTS
2½ cups ready made coconut milk
½ tsp soya sauce
2 tbsp chopped basil or coriander
salt to taste, ½ tsp brown sugar

1. Grind all the ingredients of paste with the water in which the chillies were soaked, to a very fine red paste.
2. Mix 2 tbsp oil and red paste in a microproof dish. Microwave for 3 minutes.
3. Add ½ cup of coconut milk, vegetables and microwave for 4 minutes.
4. Add the rest of the coconut milk, soya sauce and chopped basil. Mix and microwave for 4 minutes.
5. Add salt and sugar to taste. Microwave for 1 minute. Serve hot with steamed rice.

Paneer in Hot Garlic Sauce

Cottage cheese can be substituted with tofu if available.

Serves 3-4

200 gm paneer
1 capsicum - cut into tiny cubes
3 tbsp oil
20 flakes garlic - crushed (1½ tbsp)
2 dry, red chillies - broken into bits
4 tbsp tomato ketchup
2 tsp red chilli sauce
2 tsp Soya sauce
½ tsp pepper, 1 tsp salt
a pinch sugar, 2 tsp vinegar
¼ tsp ajinomoto (optional)
1½ cups water
2 tbsp cornflour mixed with ½ cup water

1. Put oil, garlic, red chilli bits, tomato ketchup, red chilli sauce, soya sauce, pepper and ajinomoto in a microproof dish. Mix well, microwave for 2 minutes.
2. Add water, salt, sugar and vinegar. Mix and microwave for 6 minutes.
3. Add cornflour paste, microwave for 3 minutes or more till slightly thick. Mix.
4. Cut paneer into 1" cubes.
5. At serving time, add paneer and capsicum to the sauce and microwave for 2 minutes. Mix well before serving. Serve with noodles or rice.

Continental & Baked Dishes

PG-80

Spinach with Cheese

Cottage cheese and spinach cooked in a thick white sauce. Enjoy it with soup and bread.

Serves 4

4 cups chopped spinach (400 gm)
1 tsp chopped garlic
2 tbsp butter
1¾ cups milk
3 tbsp flour
¾ tsp freshly ground pepper
200 gm paneer (cottage cheese) - cut into ½" cubes
¾- 1 tsp salt or to taste

1. Wash spinach leaves discarding the stems.
2. Chop and wash again. Drain water.
3. Microwave butter for 30 seconds in a microproof dish.
4. Add chopped garlic and spinach. Mix well and microwave covered for 5 minutes.
5. Add maida and mix well. Microwave for 30 seconds.
6. Add milk and mix well with a beater, so that no lumps remain. Microwave for 3 minutes.
7. Add cottage cheese, salt and freshly ground pepper. Microwave for 2 minutes. Serve with garlic bread.

Vegetable au Gratin

Mixed vegetables baked in a cheese sauce topped with bread crumbs and tomato slices.

Picture on page 4   *Serves 8*

WHITE SAUCE
4 tbsp butter, 4 tbsp maida (plain flour)
2½ cups milk, salt, pepper to taste
1 tbsp tomato ketchup

VEGETABLES
10-15 french beans - cut into ¼" pieces
2 carrots - cut into small cubes
½ small cauliflower - cut into ½" florets
½ cup shelled peas
1 medium potato - cut into small cubes
½ of small ghiya (bottle gourd) - peeled and cut into small cubes (1 cup)

TOPPING
¼ cup bread crumbs
1 tomato - sliced

1. To prepare the sauce, melt butter for 50 seconds in a microproof dish.
2. Add flour, salt, pepper, tomato ketchup. Microwave for 30 seconds.
3. Add milk. Mix well. Microwave for 6 minutes. Keep sauce aside.
4. Wash vegetables and put in a microproof deep bowl with 1 tsp salt and ¼ cup water. Microwave covered for 5 minutes.
5. Mix vegetables with the prepared sauce. Add salt if required. Microwave for 3 minutes or till sauce turns thick and coats the vegetables.
6. Arrange tomato slices over it. Sprinkle bread crumbs.
7. Set microwave oven at 200°C using the oven (convection) mode and press start to preheat oven. Put the vegetables inside the hot oven and re-set the preheated oven again at 200°C for 30 minutes. Bake till golden brown. Serve hot.

Stuffed Tomatoes

Tomatoes stuffed with cottage cheese mixed with some tomato ketchup and chilli sauce.

Serves 6-8

5 large or 8 small sized tomatoes
100 gm cottage cheese (paneer) - mashed roughly (1 cup)
50 gm grated cheese (½ cup)
½ cup onion - chopped fine
½ cup boiled peas or corn
2 tbsp tomato ketchup
2 tbsp chilli sauce
½ tsp salt
½ tsp garam masala
1 tsp amchoor (dried mango powder)

GARNISH
a few coriander leaves

1. Cut tomatoes into 2 halves if big or leave whole if small. Remove pulp and keep inverted for 3-4 minutes.
2. Mix all other ingredients gently in a bowl, taking care not to mash the paneer.
3. Spoon filling into tomato halves and arrange in a ring on a microproof plate. Microwave at combi mode (micro+grill) for 5 minutes.
4. Allow to stand for 2 minutes. Serve hot garnished with coriander leaves.

Macaroni Alfredo

Macaroni with vegetables cooked in cheese sauce. Tastes even better if grilled till golden brown.

Serves 5-6

1 cup uncooked macaroni
100 gm mushrooms - sliced
50-100 gm baby corns - sliced (optional)
2 tbsp butter, 1 tsp oregano
1 onion or 2 spring onions - chopped along with the green parts
2½ tbsp flour (maida)
1¾ cups milk
¾ tsp salt, or to taste, ½ tsp pepper
½ tsp red chilli flakes
100 gm mozerrela cheese - grated
2 tbsp bread crumbs
some tomato slices and chopped parsley

1. Put 1½ cups of water and 1 tsp oil in a deep microproof bowl. Microwave uncovered for 3 minutes.
2. Add macaroni. Mix. Microwave uncovered for 5 minutes. Let it stand in hot water for 4-5 minutes. Drain and wash well with cold water.
3. In another microproof flat dish, microwave·butter for 30 seconds.
4. Add oregano, spring onions, mushrooms and baby corns Microwave uncovered for 5 minutes.
5. Add flour. Mix well and microwave uncovered for 30 seconds.
6. Add milk, salt, pepper and chilli flakes Mix and microwave uncovered for 6 minutes, stirring once in between. Microwave for 1-2 minutes more if the sauce does not turn thick.
7. Add macaroni and ½ of grated cheese. Mix well. Sprinkle bread crumbs. Arrange tomato, coriander and the left over grated cheese.
8. At serving time, grill for 10-12 minutes or more till the top turns golden.

Bean Casserole

Red kidney beans and cauliflower baked in a creamy cheese sauce.

Serves 6   *Picture on page 93*

1¼ cups boiled rajmah (red kidney beans)
1 onion - chopped
4 cups finely chopped cauliflower
3 tomatoes
2½ tbsp tomato ketchup
1 tsp Worcestershire sauce
1½ cups (150 gm) grated cheese
½ cup cream
2 tbsp oil
salt and pepper to taste

1. Put the tomatoes on a microproof plate and microwave for 3 minutes. Remove peel after they cool. Chop finely.
2. Keep onions, cauliflower and 2 tbsp oil in a microproof dish. Mix well and microwave for 6 minutes.
3. Add 1 tsp salt and ½ tsp pepper. Add tomatoes, boiled rajmah, ketchup and worcestershire sauce. Mix well. Check salt and pepper.
4. Add half of the grated cheese.
5. Mix the other half of the cheese with cream. Add ¼ tsp salt and ¼ tsp pepper. Pour cream over the vegetables and spread gently.
6. Set microwave oven at 180°C using the oven (convection) mode and press start to preheat oven. Put the vegetables inside the hot oven and re-set the preheated oven again at 180°C for 25 minutes. Bake till golden brown. Serve hot.

Hungarian Paneer

Cottage cheese slices layered with vegetables, topped with a creamy tomato sauce flavoured with oregano.

Serves 8

700-800 gm paneer - cut into a long, thick slab (7" long and 2" thick, approx.)

FILLING (MIX TOGETHER)
¾ cup grated carrot
50 gm pizza cheese + 50 gm cheddar cheese - grated (1 cup)
¼ tsp salt and ¼ tsp freshly ground pepper
½ tsp oregano, or to taste

HUNGARIAN SAUCE
5 tomatoes
6 tbsp ready made tomato puree
2 tbsp oil, 1 tsp crushed garlic
4 tbsp cream
1 tsp oregano
½ tsp salt and ¼ tsp pepper, or to taste

1. For sauce, prick tomatoes with a fork. Put on a microproof plate and microwave for 3 minutes. Remove peel. Blend to a puree after they cool down.
2. Put oil, garlic, 6 tbsp readymade puree, prepared tomato puree, oregano, salt and pepper in a microproof bowl. Mix and microwave for 7 minutes.
3. Mix cream. Keep the sauce aside.
4. Cut paneer into 3 pieces lengthwise, of equal thickness. Sprinkle salt and pepper on both sides of each slice of paneer.
5. In a shallow rectangular serving dish, put ¼ of the prepared sauce.
6. Place a paneer slab on the sauce.
7. Spread ½ of the filling on it.
8. Press another piece of paneer on it.
9. Again put the filling on it. Cover with the last piece of paneer. Press. Pour sauce all over to cover top and sides completely.
10. Grate cheese on top. Sprinkle some oregano or pepper. To serve, microwave for 3 minutes.

Rice-Vegetable Ring

Saucy vegetables surrounded by a ring of rice mixed with green herbs.

Serves 5-6   *Picture on cover*

RICE (MIX TOGETHER)
2 cups cooked rice
¼ cup chopped parsley or coriander
salt and lemon juice to taste

OTHER INGREDIENTS
2 tbsp butter
100 gm baby corns - sliced
2 cups finely chopped spinach
2½ tbsp flour (maida)
2 cups milk
¾ tsp salt, 1 tsp pepper, 1½ tsp oregano
½-1 cup grated mozzarella cheese (50-100 gm)
some tomato slices and black olives

1. Melt butter in a microproof dish for 40 seconds.
2. Add oregano, spinach and baby corns Microwave uncovered for 5 minutes.
3. Add flour. Mix well and microwave uncovered for 1 minute.
4. Add milk, salt, 2 tbsp cheese and pepper. Mix. Microwave uncovered for 5 minutes. Keep vegetables aside.
5. Spread parsley rice in a greased dish. Push rice toward the edges of the dish to get a rice border.
6. Sprinkle some cheese on it. Leaving aside the border of rice put the vegetables in the center portion of the dish, such that the rice border forms a ring around the vegetables.
7. Arrange tomato slices around the vegetables and sprinkle the left over grated cheese. Sprinkle olives.
8. To serve, microwave for 4 minutes or grill in the oven for 15 minutes.

PG-88

Gajar ka Halwa

Carrot halwah made in very little fat and in a jiffy too.

Serves 5-6

½ kg carrots - grated
1½ cups milk
½ cup sugar - powdered, or to taste
½ cup (100 gms) khoya - grated
2-3 tbsp desi ghee
some chopped nuts like almonds, raisins (kishmish) etc.

1. Mix grated carrots and milk in a big deep bowl.
2. Microwave uncovered for 15 minutes. Mix once after 5 minutes.
3. Add sugar and khoya. Mix well.
4. Microwave for 10 minutes uncovered.
5. Add ghee. Mix well. Microwave for 7 minutes. Mix chopped nuts. Serve hot or cold decorated with nuts.

Phirni

Rice pudding flavoured with green cardamoms and topped with nuts.

Serves 4

3½ cups milk
¼ cup rice - soaked for 2-3 hours and ground to a fine paste
¼ cup powdered sugar, or to taste
1 tsp kewra or rose water - (optional) or a drop of kewra essence
seeds of 2-3 chhoti illaichi (green cardamom) - powdered
varak (silver leaf)
5-6 green pistas - sliced thinly
2 almonds - sliced into thin long pieces

1. Soak rice in a little water for 2-3 hours. Grind in the mixer with a little water to a very fine paste.
2. In a dish mix ground rice and milk.
3. Microwave uncovered for 6 minutes. Stir with a wire whisk, after every minute otherwise lumps will form. Break lumps if any.
4. Add sugar. Mix well. Microwave uncovered for 3 minutes, stirring in-between.
5. Mix well. Cool. Add rose/kewra water and illaichi powder. Pour in individual bowls.
6. Decorate with varak, nuts and illaichi powder. Serve chilled after 2-3 hours.

Chocolate Walnut Cake (Eggless)

Serves 6   *Picture on back cover*

½ tin condensed milk (milkmaid)
½ cup milk
½ cup butter (75 gm)
1½ tbsp powdered sugar
100 gm (1cup) maida (palin flour)
¼ cup cocoa
¾ tsp level soda-bi-carb (mitha soda)
¾ tsp level baking powder
1 tsp vanilla essence
2-3 tbsp chopped walnuts - mixed with 1 tsp maida

TOPPING
some ready-made chocolate sauce
2-3 walnuts - halves

1. Sift maida, cocoa, soda-bi-carb and baking powder.
2. Mix sugar and butter. Beat with an electric hand mixer till fluffy.
3. Add milkmaid and beat some more, for about 2 minutes.
4. Add milk and essence. Add maida. Beat well for about 3-4 minutes, till the mixture is smooth and light.
5. Mix walnuts mixed with 1 tsp of maida and add to the cake batter.
6. Grease a deep, big bowl. Transfer mixture to the bowl. Microwave for 5 minutes. The cake will appear wet after 5 minutes, but just let it be undisturbed in the microwave for 10 minutes. (Do not microwave more)
7. Remove cake from bowl on the serving plate. Pour some chocolate sauce on the hot cake. Sprinkle some more walnuts if you like. Serve.

Vanilla Cake

For vanilla cake, add ¼ cup cornflour to maida and remove ¼ cup cocoa. The rest of the recipe is the same.

Eggless Cake with Mocha Icing

A quick microwaved chocolate cake topped with chocolate icing flavoured with coffee.

Picture on facing page   Serves 6

½ tin condensed milk (milk-maid)
½ cup milk, ½ cup (75 gm) butter
1½ tbsp powdered sugar
100 gms (1 cup) maida (plain flour)
¼ cup cocoa, ¾ tsp level soda-bicarb
¾ tsp level baking powder
1 tsp vanilla essence

MOCHA GLAZE ICING
4 tbsp cocoa powder, 2 tbsp butter - softened
1 tsp coffee
1 cup icing sugar - sifted
2-3 tbsp chopped walnuts (akhrot)

TO SOAK
¼ cup coke or any other cola drink

1. Sift maida with cocoa, soda-bi-carb and baking powder. Keep aside.
2. Mix sugar and butter. Beat till very fluffy. Add milk-maid. Beat well.
3. Add milk and essence. Add maida. Beat well for 3-4 minutes till the mixture is smooth and light. Transfer to a big, greased deep dish of 8" diameter.
4. Microwave for 5 minutes. Let it cool.
5. Cut cake into 2 and soak with cola drink.
6. For the icing, microwave 4 tbsp water in a bowl for 1 minute. Add coffee and mix. Add cocoa and butter to it and mix well. Return to microwave and microwave at 70% power for 1 minute or till butter melts. Gradually add the sifted icing sugar. Mix well.
7. Glaze the cake with the icing, making peaks with the spoon. Decorate it with walnuts.
8. Refrigerate until glaze is set. Serve with ice cream.

*Bean Casserole: Recipe on pa** 85* ➤
*Eggless Cake with Mocha Ic** j* ➤

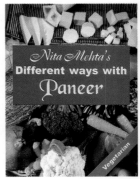

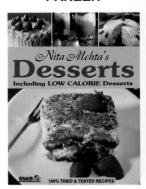

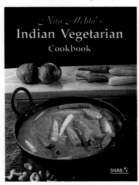

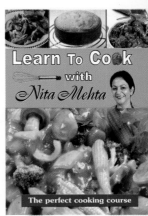

BEST SELLERS BY *Nita Mehta*

PUNJABI
Khaana

The Best of
CHICKEN & PANEER

The Best of
NON-VEGETARIAN

BAKES & CAKES
Baking with Confidence!

ALL TIME FAVOURITE
SNACKS

CHINESE
Vegetarian Cuisine

PANEER All the Way

Dal & Roti

Taste of Rajasthan

ZERO OIL
Cookbook

Vegetarian
CURRIES

Vegetarian
Sandwiches

MORE PANEER

JHATPAT KHAANA

LOSE WEIGHT

MORE SNACK

MICROWAVE Non-Veg.

Favourite NON-VEG.

The Best of MUTTON

ITALIAN Non-Veg.

BEST SELLING COOKBOOKS BY  SNAB

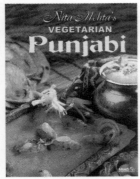

Vegetarian PUNJABI

CHINESE cooking for the Indian kitchen

ITALIAN cooking for the Indian kitchen

Simply Delicious CURRIES

The Best of CHICKEN & PANEER

SUBZIYAAN

TANDOORI cooking in the OVEN

Tempting SNACKS

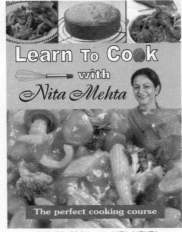

LEAR TO COOK with NITA MEHTA

Flavours of INDIAN Cooking

Oats Breakfast Cookbook

Leran to Cook CHOCOLATE

Learn Food Styling, Garnishing & Table Laying

Leran to Cook PIZZA & PASTA

Leran to Cook LEBANESE

BEST SELLING COOKBOOKS BY  SNAB

Everyday Khaana

All Time Favourite Snacks

Chaawal

Continental Vegetarian

51 DIET Recipes

Mexican vegetarian

Tandoori Cooking - Veg

Taste of Delhi

Eggless Desserts

Paranthas & Rice for Kids

Italian Vegetarian

Paneer All the Way

Low Calorie Snacks

More Snacks

Soup & Salad

Vegetarian Dishes

Menus from Around the world

Different ways with Vegetables

Vegetarian Sandwiches

Green Vegetables

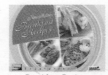
Breakfast Recipes

Paneer Recipes

Cook in Minutes

Indian Low Fat

Snacks & Chaat

Pasta & Corn

Eggless Oven Recipes

Soups Salads & Starters

Tiffin recipes for Children

Chinese Veg. Recipes

Chatpati Chaat

The Art of Baking

Cakes & Cookies

Vegetarian Recipes

Zero Oil Recipes

Pressure Cooking

Mughlai Vegetarian

Vegetarian Curries

Microwave Vegetarian

More Desserts